WHAT PEOPLE SAY AB
ANGEL DOGS METHOD

Patty and Hal Earnhardt: "Eileen is very professional and knowledgeable with our animals. They looked forward to her coming in the mornings. There was a dramatic improvement with their obedience and overall behavior."

Amanda and Leonard Davis: (NFL player for the Dallas Cowboys). They have six dogs all trained by Eileen. "Mia is a new woman! She was the worst dog. Thanks! CeCe has become more outgoing and less apprehensive about things and commands."

Darlene Farnsworth: "Simply amazing. We were at the point of possibly parting with Bella but after just one session with Eileen. What a difference! She is a different dog. I love the calm and professional manner in which she trains. Actually she trained us as well. She is simply the best! She far exceeded our expectations."

Pat Lawson is involved with a national service dog group: "I have been associated with Eileen Tonick for 10 years regarding her services as a dog trainer. She successfully raised two puppies who both are now serving as Guide Dogs for their blind partners. This is exceptionally noteworthy as only about one third of the puppies raised to be Guide Dogs graduate to become partnered with someone who is visually impaired. A good deal of the success of a potential guide dog depends upon the puppy raiser. Eileen was outstanding in her work with these two. I have also had the pleasure of experience with Eileen and her company, Angel Dogs Training. Our local service dog group has taken advantage of Eileen's dog training expertise on several occasions. Without exception, all of our trainees who entered her training class passed their AKC Canine Good Citizen tests. Eileen's knowledge of dog training and her inherit knowledge of dog psychology have been much appreciate by our group."

Kate Hope: "Our dog has calmed down considerably since beginning his training. Because Eileen has taught us to take control, rather than let Jake have the control over the house. We have all benefited."

Andrea Streed: "Techniques were excellent. Max had problems with aggression and Eileen definitely helped. We will definitely keep up with the training we learned."

Dana Morrison: "She has great expertise with animals and guiding owners in supporting their dogs. I have no prior training experience and after this class we are ready to pass the Delta class. Eileen is awesome with animals and their owners."

David Zamora: "There is great benefit to both Pepper and myself with the training skills/tips. "Very effective instruction."

Janet Margrave: "Blue learned a lot. The training techniques were gentle but effective."

Erin Dewan: "This class was awesome. I have a different dog. He's incredible now and I feel confident in controlling him."

Jane Anderson: "I thought they (the training methods) were great! Very easy to understand and thorough. I appreciated the time Eileen always took to answer any questions I had, always making sure I understood. A wonderful experience that will make my life with my dogs so much better and enjoyable."

All Dogs Are Angels At Heart

Make your dog an "Angel Dog" in 5 weeks, a fun
and informative book for kids and adults

by

Eileen Tonick, MA, IACP
&
Mickey McGovern

authorHOUSE®

AuthorHouse™
1663 Liberty Drive, Suite 200
Bloomington, IN 47403
www.authorhouse.com
Phone: 1-800-839-8640

First published by AuthorHouse   1/14/2008

ISBN: 978-1-4343-5109-8 (sc)

Library of Congress Control Number: 2007909033

Printed in the United States of America
Bloomington, Indiana

This book is printed on acid-free paper.

www.angeldogstraining.net

Cover Photos by Pat Lawson

Internal Photos and Filters by Mickey McGovern

DEDICATION

To my Phil my husband of thirty years. Thank you for your support, encouragement, ideas and love.

To Timber, Tank, Tommie, Bebe and all the other dogs that bring joy and unconditional love into my life.

FOREWORD

I talked my sister into letting me help her write this book because I knew it would take a lot of work to get it the way she wanted it.

There are quotes here from people whose dogs were acting out and driving them loony. These desperate owners called Eileen because she is well known in these parts or because their veterinarian or a friend recommended her. She jumps in her blue jeep and drives to their house. She evaluates the dog and the owner. It's usually the owner's fault I've discovered. She tells them, "This is a very cool dog. He's awesome. We can get him straightened around in no time." The relief they feel is huge. I've seen Eileen turn out of control dogs into angels in seconds.

After some basic obedience training the dogs and the owners often attend an "agility" or "therapy dog" class taught by Eileen. The dogs are excited and happy to be there with the other dogs. It's like camp or a festival. The owners fall in love with their dogs again. The dogs, of course, always love their owners, no matter what. Amazing creatures.

Everyone should read this book. You should especially read it before you get a dog so you know exactly what's involved. I'm not only talking to the adults I'm talking to the kids too.

Mickey McGovern has worked in the Hollywood film industry for fifteen years as a writer and a visual effects producer. But more importantly she's Eileen Tonick's sister.

INTRODUCTION

Hi. My name is Eileen Tonick, MA, IACP (International Association of Canine Professionals). I'm an expert in dog behaviors, a dog trainer and a former evaluator for Delta Society and AKC Canine Good Citizen. I have dedicated my life to the well being of dogs because owning and training a dog is an exciting, fun experience and because my biggest heart break is millions of dogs are put to sleep each year simply because they don't behave. That's a terrible reason. I'm determined to stop the euthanasia of dogs any way that I can. One of those ways is to teach your dog to be a good citizen.

I've been a trainer for fifteen years and in that time I've developed what I refer to as "Angel Dogs Training." This method is all about being calm, patient, consistent and loving. It's easy to master. You can train your dog in five weeks to be a well behaved, good friend.

Puppies scamper into the family home as a pet and companion for children. "It's your puppy you take care of him," is the rule. Parents have jobs, work around the house and raise their children. There's not enough time in the day for the puppy too. But children don't have a clue about how to take care of and train a dog. This book will fix that!

The puppy can grow into a neglected dog who is a pest for attention. He's chased out into the back yard where he's fed once a day if someone thinks about it. He becomes destructive, depressed and unhappy. He becomes unhealthy. Finally he's taken to the pound and if he's lucky he's adopted.

It's frustrating when you ask your dog to do something and they refuse. Those days are over. This book will give you some insight into how dogs think. From now on your best buddy will happily follow your commands.

Dogs are great company. They love to hang out with you. They will protect you if you are threatened. Children love my dog, Timber, because she's so sweet and well behaved. They always say to me, "I want your dog."

They depend on you for survival: food, water, shelter and affection. That's all they really think about. "Where's my food? Where's my water? Give me a treat." You can be proud of them and love them back. A well trained, well behaved dog is easy to love.

Kids pick the coolest name they can think of for their dog. They should keep that kind of attitude going every day. There are over 73 million dogs in the United States. That's a lot of dogs to take care of.

You can read this book straight through or you can go to the chapters that apply to you right now. Each chapter is easy and fast to read. It's just the facts and some good stories. The main thing is that you learn how to take care of your best friend.

CONTENTS

Chapter One

Tools for Training your Dog.

Properly trained, a man can be dog's best friend.
– Corey Ford

You don't want your dog to get away from you…ever! Keep him on a leash when you go out because he will get so focused on something that interests him he won't hear you when you call.

Proper tools make training easier. I've discovered some important facts about these tools.

I prefer:
- A **six-foot leather leash** is standard for training. Unlike nylon, leather doesn't cut or burn your hands if your dog pulls hard. A leather leash also allows for a good, firm grip.
- A **head collar** slides over your dog's nose and in back of his ears. It makes training easier because you have control of the dog's head. Read the instruction and view the CD that comes with the head collar.

- A **body harness** is a tool for a dog with a short nose (English Bulldogs, Pugs). The dog can pull and drag you but you can master it with practice.
- A **flat collar** carries the dog's identification, the dog's name and your phone number only. If you use a flat collar for training, beware that it can cause throat and neck injury.
- You also need a **rabies tag and a chip identification tag**. A veterinarian injects the chip into your dog's neck just above the shoulders. It contains an ID number and when scanned brings up information to find the owner.

The Gentle Leader Headcollar® is one of my favorite training tools. I've used it successfully for years. When I work with dogs, I take the role as dominant leader and the dog takes the role as calm submissive. This means that when I ask the dog to do something he does it. The Gentle Leader® is just one of the ways I become the dominant leader. I like this tool because it gives children and adults with limited strength leverage and control. As with any training tool there is a proper way to use it. Follow the instructions.

I prefer not to use the following:
- **Chokers** – chain or nylon - Be careful using this tool. Seek the advice of a dog trainer.
- **Prong Collars** – I don't use this tool often. I have a client who has MS (Muscular Sclerosis) and doesn't have enough body strength so we decided to use a prong collar. Improperly used or improperly adjusted it can injure the dog's neck.

- **Electric Collars** – Avoid this collar unless a professional teaches you how to use one.

THE KIM AND LUKE STORY:

Luke is a 150 pound, big, strong St. Bernard. He joined Kim's family when he was 5 years old. Other families gave up on Luke because they didn't know how to control him. Kim called me after one of my clients told her about Angel Dogs and how successful I was training their dog.

I watched Luke drag Kim from one bush to another and fling her into the air (Kim weights about 100 pounds) like a rag doll. "Do you feel like you have control of Luke?" I asked.

She laughed and replied, "Not in the least!"

I recommended a Gentle Leader® and gave her the reasons I wanted to try this training tool.

Kim said, "I'm so frustrated I'll be willing to try almost anything."

Within minutes Luke was walking a calm submissive walk. He adjusted immediately and became aware of my needs and wants instead of his own agenda, which was sniffing the bushes.

Kim took over and for the first time felt like she had control. During the second lesson Kim walked Luke in the neighborhood and a local park. There were plenty of distractions but Kim stayed in control. Distractions are everywhere and it is important that your dog pay attention to you.

Kim began to understand how to work with Luke and how to help him become a dog that people want to be around, instead of avoid.

- **Assertive Calm** – You need to be calm and firm in your requests of your dog. Don't back down. Don't become impatient. Don't hurt your dog to get them to do what you want.

- **Neutral Body Energy** – Always remain cool and collected. Don't become stressed and display impatience, apprehension or anger.
- **Submissive Calm** – The dog must give in to your will calmly.
- **Everyone must be calm all the time.**

EILEEN AND LUKE

Chapter Two

Food, Water, Bedding, Crate, Toys, Food as Love.

Every puppy should have a boy.
– Erma Bombeck

BEBE'S STORY:

"My name is Bebe. I'm a cute female Jack Russell Terrier. I live in a big house with my mistress, my master, two little boys and a big boy. My biggest worry every day is that I have what I need to survive. I scavenge for food all day. I looovvvvee human food. Yummy. Steak, potato chips, cookies, ice-cream and mostly I love chocolate. I have a story to tell you later about that.

The little boys, Colten and Hayden, fill my water dishes to the top every day. Colten feeds me one half a cup of dog food recommended by my veterinarian twice a day.

Sometimes my mistress treats me with a hot dog or some chicken or some steak. I gobble up my dog food with gravy or spaghetti sauce on it. I'm a little fat. My trainer frowns. She taped a picture of a cute

Jack Russell on the refrigerator door to remind my mistress how slim I should be. She also gave her this tip: put some dog kibble in a baggie and use that as a treat.

The family buys me toys so I can play. I chase balls. I wrestle with toys that have a squeaky so when I bite them they make a great noise. I snuggle with stuffed animals. I carry one around. My mistress calls it, "My baby." Playing with my toys keeps me busy and out of trouble.

I sleep on the cool floor in the laundry room and I have a cozy crate with a rug and a blanket. My master forbids me to sleep in the little boy's beds even if I whine and cry.

If I sleep in someone's bed and I stand over them I think that I'm high up in the pecking order. I'm the dog and all family members are higher than me. Dogs live by pack mentality.

Pack Mentality has a hierarchy (one dog is in a higher position than another dog). The older and stronger dogs rule over the younger and weaker dogs. The father and mother are above the kids and the kids are above the animals. If the cat hangs around I chase it. It spits at me and scares me away. I'm trying to figure out if I'm above the cat!

At Easter time I stumbled upon a bag of dark chocolate candies wrapped in colored foil. I stole them like the little thief I am, snuck under the bed in the guestroom, unwrapped and ate every one. They were sooo good.

Later I felt terrible. I pooped on the floor. My master picked me up and put me in the backyard. He was upset that I pooped in the house but as he cleaned it up he noticed that it smelled like chocolate.

He called my trainer at Angel Dogs. She said, "Chocolate is very bad. Take Bebe to the veterinarian right now." My master grabbed me up and jumped in his big white car. He drove quickly to the veterinarian. I've never seen him that upset before.

She examined me and put an IV in my little leg. I would have to stay in the hospital all night. My master didn't want to leave me but he went home to tell the family I would be fine. Phew. That was close. The next day when my master picked me up he had to pay a large amount of money. Now they hide the candy. The little boys remind themselves I can't have candy and ice-cream. Bummer.

My family loves me and they like to show their love by giving me all the good treats they like to eat especially since I'm so good at begging with my pretty brown eyes.

To show me affection and reward give me clean water every day, good food but not too much, some doggie snacks and a clean safe cozy place to sleep. Then I will be happy, healthy, and safe and will feel secure and loved. It's like saying, "You're a good dog Bebe."

HAYDEN AND BEBE

CHAPTER THREE

The Veterinarian – Dog's Health.

There is honor in being a dog. – Aristotle

I want my dogs to have a great veterinarian, one that I can depend on and trust. My dog's doctor is as important as my personal doctor. Get recommendations from other dog owners or from your trainer.

You need someone to examine your dog regularly and be there in an emergency.

- A puppy must have a series of vaccines in the first year.
- **Shots/Vaccines** – Your veterinarian will advise you on the vaccines your puppy needs in your particular state and will provide you with a vaccine record.
- **Deworm your puppies** – It is important for their health.
- **A fecal check up** is how a veterinarian checks for worms or other conditions.
- **A simple examination** – The veterinarian checks temperature, heart, lungs, bones, teeth, and ears.

- Puppies get **ear infections** so watch for this.
- Have a **heart worm exam** and use monthly preventive medication recommended by your veterinarian.
- **Do flea and tick prevention.**
- When your dog turns a year old she will go to the veterinarian once a year unless she has a health condition that requires special care.
- **Food** – The veterinarian will recommend a diet to keep your puppy healthy and trim. Stick to it.

Their teeth are as important as yours.

- Get a doggy tooth brush and doggy toothpaste from your local pet supply store or your veterinarian.
- Don't use human toothpaste.
- Give him a chew toy to help with dental care.
- Schedule an annual teeth cleaning with your veterinarian.

Get your dog neutered or spayed. These are the reasons:

- Keep the pet population down. We have millions of dogs in shelters in this country. It is a disgrace how many dogs they kill each year.
- Prevent male dogs from wandering. They look for female dogs to mate with.
- Stop your dog from marking (peeing) in your house. They will mark on the rug, your bed and on your drapes. They want other dogs to know this is their territory.
- Sometimes neutering will help keep aggression down.
- Stop them from attempting to mount people.
- To prevent some forms of cancer.

Hip Dysplasia:

In my mom's generation, seventy years ago, there was minimal hip dysplasia. But now there are so many bad breeding practices that we are seeing more and more cases in big and small dogs. Even Jack Russell Terriers are showing more hip dysplasia than in the past.

Here are the signs you should be looking for:

- Weakness and sensitivity in the hip area.
- Your dog walks funny, limps, becomes lame, has trouble sitting, standing or lying down or even has trouble resting.
- Your dog doesn't lie in the normal position and can't stretch out his hindquarters.
- Your dog may even whimper when someone touches his hips, when he sits or when he lies down.

Preventive Care:

- Take your dog to a veterinarian for x-rays.
- Give puppies a calorie-restricted diet. Fat dogs will have more trouble with their joints.
- Provide quality food but not growth formulas.
- Your veterinarian may recommend food, medication or vitamins.
- Do not run your dog long distances until they are two years old.
- Do not let your dog jump from high places or rough house with other dogs or people.
- You may have to take your dog to an orthopedic specialist for surgery.
- Do not breed your dog if they have hip dysplasia or any serious medical conditions.
- Do not buy a puppy if the breeder cannot prove the breeding pair of dogs did not have hip dysplasia for three generations.

- OFA and Penn Hip are x-ray readings to rate the severity of a dog's hips.

TYPHOON'S STORY:

Typhoon was a large breed American Bulldog. When we got Typhoon we were not aware of hip dysplasia but after this heart breaking experience I became acutely aware of this type of joint disease.

We brought Typhoon home when he was 7 weeks old. He whimpered if we picked him up or put pressure on his hind end. He would lie down tucking his hip's way up under his stomach at a strange angle. When he was six months old he was x-rayed and the veterinarian told me that Typhoon had bad hips. He suggested that I take him to an orthopedic specialist.

The orthopedic surgeon recommended two types of surgery. They were both expensive, in the thousands of dollars. He wanted us to limit Typhoon's running and jumping to avoid stress on his joints. He suggested swimming as a low impact exercise. He put Typhoon on a medication called Rimadyl® and added vitamin and minerals to his diet.

We kept his weight down and did what the veterinarian told us so we could keep Typhoon comfortable throughout his life.

Be careful here:
- Talk to your veterinarian about any problems common to a breed before you buy that breed.
- Do your research.
- Do not buy your puppy from a puppy mill. A puppy mill is a place that breeds dogs quickly for sale. Some of them are not careful in their breeding practices.

- A good breeder will share any medical history about the puppy's ancestors.
- If you rescue a dog from the pound, something that I love to see, have your veterinarian check the dog over carefully.

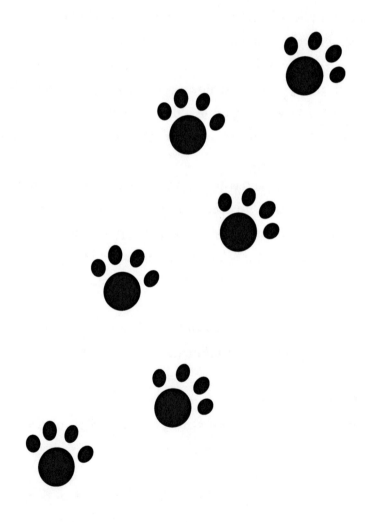

CHAPTER FOUR

Travel Safety.

Dogs are not our whole life, but they make our lives whole.
– Roger Caras

There are sad stories about dogs that are hurt or killed while traveling. Don't put your dog in the bed of a truck. They can fall or jump out.

A dog gets dehydrated in the back of a truck or can burn her feet in the hot weather. Make traveling in the bed of a truck safer by using a pet carrier and then securing that carrier.

Watch the weather. You don't want your pet in the bed of a truck if it's hot, cold or if it's raining.

Traveling safely in a car:
- If your dog is in a carrier, strap it down.
- If you don't use a carrier use a dog seat belt. Buy one at your local pet supply store.
- Do not leave your dog unattended in a car when it's hot or cold. A hot car can reach temperatures that are

dangerously high. A freezing car can also harm your dog.

- Don't hold your dog in your lap while riding in a car. If the car stops suddenly your dog will fly out of your arms. Air bags will go off and injure your dog.
- Bring plenty of water for your dog.

BEBE'S TRAVEL STORY:

"Hi. It's me Bebe again. Some dogs don't like to travel in a car. It makes them sick and nervous. I love to travel in a car. My master and mistress takes the two little boys and the big boy on camping trips. I get to go too. Recently we went to Dog Town to camp for four days. I'm not kidding. It was Dog Town in Arizona. It's right outside Williams. They took a dog to Dog Town. Ha-Ha. That's funny. The campgrounds are named after the prairie dogs that once lived around the lake.

They put me in a doggie seat belt in the backseat of the Yukon. I love the sound of the engine and the motion of the car. I fell asleep in about two minutes. I slept the whole three hours while the little boys watched a movie on the DVD player.

My master is a great driver so I don't worry about an accident. I can't sit on anyone's lap while the car is going, especially in the front seat. If we had an accident and the air bag went off it could hurt me. It is as important to my family that I be as safe in the car as the children. They also don't want me jumping all over the place. That's irritating and distracting for the driver.

When we got to Dog Town I felt good from my three hour nap. I ran around the campsite and the woods. I slept in the camper at night. It was great. I loved it.

CHAPTER FIVE

Grooming

A good dog bath is like a rainy day. – Eileen Tonick
Anybody who doesn't know what soap tastes like never washed a
dog. – Franklin P. Jones

Grooming is important. Make sure your dog is clean and eliminate any bugs on her. Grooming is a good way to bond with her.

Brush your dog daily and give her a bath at least once a month. Don't wash your dog too much it can dry out her skin and make her itch.

Do it like this:
- Use warm water, a good doggie shampoo, a clean towel to dry your dog and a brush or comb.
- Inspect for fleas and ticks.
- Check your dog's ears for dirt or infections. Clean her ears with an ear cleaning solution made for dogs and cotton balls. Do not use que-tips.

- Check her teeth and brush them three or four times a week.
- Check her feet for foxtails or burrs.
- Make sure her toe nails and dew claws are clipped. Be careful clipping her nails. Don't clip too close. Use a nail clipper made for dogs.
- If you don't want to clip your dog's nails or if the dog doesn't want you to clip her nails, take her to a groomer or your veterinarian. They have experience clipping nails.
- Give your dog frequent brushings to prevent knots and collect loose hair.
- Your dog will love these times if you make it fun and you give her a treat.
- Some breeds go to a groomer to get a special haircut.
- Make sure your dog likes the groomer so their visit is fun and enjoyable. Some groomers will come to your house in a van and wash and groom you dog right there in your driveway.

TIMBER'S BATH STORY:

"I hate baths. I do. Keep me away from the tub. I don't like swimming in the pool or in the river or in the ocean. I'll drink water but that is all I want to do with it.

I live in a place that's hot in the summer so my mistress takes me outside to give me a bath with the hose. She turns on the water with a gentle stream. I don't want to get wet, please don't get me wet, yuck! But she doesn't listen. She likes a sweet smelling, clean dog. I'm doomed.

She says, "stand" and I do because I am trained. She gets me all wet with the hose. I try to sneak away but she holds me by my collar and says, "stay." Then she says, "good girl" in a nice pleasant voice. It makes me feel special and loved. She squirts some dog shampoo on me and rubs. I like that part. She rubs and rubs me all over. Then she gets the hose again and rinses me off. She rinses and rinses. It's hot so it feels good but I'm happy when she turns off that darn water.

She grabs a towel and rubs me some more. When I'm kind of dry she takes a big brush and brushes me all over. She checks my paws. She gets in between my toes looking for burrs and stickers. The whole time she is telling me what a good dog I am and gives me one of her special smiles.

She takes her clippers and trims my toe nails and that little nail on my leg. I'm done. Yipee! I look good. I run around showing everyone how good I look. "Smell me! Smell me! Don't I smell great? I think I smell great."

I roll in the grass. My mistress yells at me, "You better not roll in the dirt!" And to make sure she puts me in the house until I'm dry. That's when I get a treat and a "good dog" hug. She loves me. I know. I love her too."

EILEEN, COLTEN AND TIMBER

CHAPTER SIX

Before you bring a dog into the family consider this!

In order to really enjoy a dog, one doesn't merely try to train him to be semi-human. The point of it is to open oneself to the possibility of becoming partly a dog. – Edward Hoagland

Before you get a dog think about it. Think hard. Owning a dog is work and responsibility.

You can't get a dog and be sorry later. You can't give the responsibility of your dog to someone else. This is your dog and just like everything in life you take good care of what's yours.

Things to consider:

- **Veterinarian Expense** – An appointment with your veterinarian is costly. There are vaccines and exams. If your dog is hurt or eats chocolate like Bebe it will be expensive.

- **Food Expense** – Good dog food costs you money every month. If you have a little dog it costs less than feeding a large dog.
- **Training** - Basic Obedience, Agility, Flyball or any special training is important for your pet. That means training fees.
- **Supplies** – Toys, blankets, beds, brushes, shampoos, toothpaste, leashes, collars etc. In the life time of a dog you will buy a lot of these things.
- **Grooming** - Regular trips to the groomer for baths, haircuts and nail trims.
- **Things can be destroyed** – Puppies like to chew. If you leave your dog alone he can chew your shoes, furniture or your rug.
- **The amount of time you have to give your dog** – A dog requires time every day. You have to feed them, clean up after them, bathe, exercise and train them.
- **The devotion they need from you** – Your dog wants to be with you. He loves to play. You must take care of his mind, his body and his spirit every day.
- **Don't take any dog** - Choose one that suits you and your life style. A little dog might be better than a big dog. A mixed breed dog might be better for you than a pure breed.

THE NEGLECTED DOG STORY:

Bebe and Timber are loved dogs who get good care. So this story is not about them. This story is about another dog.

One day a man went to buy his little boy a dog. The boy had asked the man for a dog many times.

"You have to take care of him," said the man.

"I will," said the little boy. "I will love him and take care of him."

So, the man got the boy a pure bred puppy. The puppy cost the man a thousand dollars.

They went to the store and got the puppy supplies: a bed, brushes, bowls, toothpaste, shampoo and food. The bill was $150.

They took the puppy to the veterinarian who gave him his first series of vaccines. The visit and the vaccines cost $75.00. The puppy would have to go back for more vaccines. Each time it would cost money.

The boy loved the puppy. He fed him and played with him. But after awhile the boy wanted to go and play with his friends. He wanted to play baseball and ride his bike. He didn't want to take the puppy with him. The puppy got bigger and bigger and harder to control.

Every day when the boy came home for dinner his mother would tell him, "Feed your dog and give him clean water." But the boy ran to his room to watch television and the mother took care of the dog.

One day the boy came home and found all his comic books torn to shreds. He was mad at his puppy and he hit him. The puppy ran and hid under the bed.

"Did you take your puppy for a walk?" His mother asked. "No," said the boy. "I'm too tired."

The puppy was neglected. He acted out. The father put him in the back yard because he would destroy things in the house.

The puppy grew into a dog who did not behave well. He barked and tore up plants and drip systems in the backyard. He wanted to be in the house but then he ran around and jumped on people. He had become a large dog. He could knock people over.

The mother worried about the dog. She worried that he would do something bad or that something terrible would happen to him. Finally the father took the dog to a no-kill shelter.

This is a sad story and one that happens often. It can be avoided easily. Please remember when you ask for a puppy you must be ready to spend money on him and you must spend time with him.

One day a woman came into the pound. She saw the puppy. "That's a cute dog," she said.

"Yes," said the pound attendant. "He's a very good dog but he needs training."

"I'll take him," the woman said.

The attendant at the pound told the woman to call Angel Dogs because I'm a good trainer with a good reputation for dealing with dogs who have behavioral problems. When the woman got home she called me.

Our time together was spent discussing and resolving behavioral problems and learning basic obedience skills. There will be more about how to do this later in the book. The good news is that the dog learned quickly. Now the dog attends my agility classes and will also become a pet therapy dog. The woman is happy with the dog that she named Noche. Noche is happy with the woman. It's a perfect partnership.

THERAPY TRAINING CLASS
NOCHE AND HIS OWNER, KATHY

CHAPTER SEVEN

Rules & Boundaries and House Manners.

If you have good manners you can go anywhere and be with anyone. If you have good manners everyone likes you. Let's raise a well-mannered dog. That's what Angel Dogs is all about.
– Eileen Tonick

RULES & BOUNDARIES

You must have the respect of your dogs when they live in your home. Nothing is worse than an unruly, out of control dog. The next series of chapters will cover rules and boundaries.

The first thing I have my clients do is have a meeting with everyone in the house and make a rule and boundary list. At our next meeting we go through the list and talk about it.

Rules & Boundaries:
- Humans are above the dogs in the house.

- Let the dogs work out their pack order and respect it.
- Write the rules down and post them on the refrigerator.
- Everyone must follow them.
- Don't let the dogs run through the house or jump on the furniture. They can hurt themselves or cause damage.
- Don't let a dog jump on anyone. It could cause an injury or in a dog's mind it would mean they are your boss.
- No growling at family members or visitors.
- A dog is an animal not your baby. Dogs need us to treat them like dogs so they don't get confused. If a dog is confused about who he is he will act out.
- Plan a dog's daily schedule. Include daily exercise like a walk on a leash around the neighborhood not just down to the mail box. This will socialize your dog.
- Socializing is important. The dog must learn how to behave properly around other dogs, people and even kids on skateboards.
- Have a list of commands for the dog to follow: sit, stay, come, heel, down, leave it etc. Make sure each family member understands these commands and uses them. Use the hand signals that go with the commands. More about that in a later chapter.
- Give a task to each family member. Colten has to walk his dog daily. Hayden has to keep the dog's water bowl full.
- Don't ignore your dog. He must follow the rules and your dog can't boss around family members.

I often go to peoples' homes where the dog has taken control and the family is unhappy. Listed below are some simple rules so you can have a well-mannered dog.

Rules:

- When your dog is a puppy keep him on a leash whenever he's out of his crate. This way you can correct any bad behaviors instantly. You can stop him when he jumps on people, tries to go pee in the house, or runs in the house.

- Limit his indoor space. Baby gates are helpful.

- If you adopt an older dog keep your dog on a leash for the first week to 30 days.

- When your dog is on leash do not let him wander off by himself.

- Do not let your dog run up and down the stairs, he could hurt himself or someone on the stairs.

- Teach your dog the sit/stay command immediately.

- Teach your dog to go to his bed, do a down/stay and not leave his bed until you say so.

- Crate train your dog and have him sleep in his crate at night. See the crate as the dog's bedroom instead of a prison.

- Go out the door first. This simple rule tells your dog you are in charge. Do not let your dog crowd or push you to get through the door first.

- When you answer your door have your dog do a sit/stay while you talk to the person at your door.

- Do not let your dog become aggressive with anyone.

- Establish a dominance position with your dog. That means you are the boss.

- Feed your dog after you eat, this reinforces a dominance position.

- Use a firm tone of voice. Say, "Bebe. Sit," with strength. Don't waffle. Look straight into her eyes until she does what you say.
- If your dog is not listening to you and is being a pain there's a simple but effective way to get her attention. Get a spray bottle full of water. If she is being naughty and refuses to obey squirt her and firmly tell her "leave it." After a few squirts she will behave the second you pick up the spray bottle. This does not mean you get to squirt your dog with the spray bottle for fun. Use it only when she is intentionally ignoring you or is so caught up in what she's doing that she can't hear anything else.
- Remember to reward your dog for leaving something alone say "good dog" or give them a treat.
- Do not yell at or hit your dog.
- Learn how to redirect your dog's bad behaviors into good behaviors.
- Always leave a training session on a good note. Dogs remember how the session ended.

MY MOM'S STORY:

My mom is a small woman in her 80's and not as strong as she used to be. Everyone in the family is taller than she is.

One of my dogs, Teak, an American Bulldog, loves to greet people and some times she jumps on them. She wants to see their face.

One day my mom was walking down the hall and Teak went to greet her. Teak got excited and jumped on my mom knocking her against the wall.

I was not only concerned for my mom's safety I was embarrassed that my dog had such bad house manners. Teak had no idea that she hurt my mom she just wanted to say hi so I decided to turn this incident into a training session. My mother thought it was a great idea. I put Teak on a leash and practiced the sit/stay command. Then I had my mom give the commands until Teak would do the sit/stay for the both of us.

After Teak understood we practiced the sit/stays without the leash. Each day we would practice inside and outside the house until Teak knew that when she wants to greet someone she does not jump on them, instead she sits politely. Her good manners are rewarded with a treat, a good rub or a happy hello.

A well-mannered dog is a pleasure for you or anyone who visits your house. I have clients whose friends didn't want to come to their home because their dog was out of control. They didn't know how to get control and harmony back into their home.

Some clients thought they could love their dogs into being well-mannered. That doesn't work.

Good House Manners Tips:

- Find a good dog trainer and join a group. Being with other dogs and people will socialize them.
- Teach your dog basic obedience and respect.
- Train your dog daily and challenge them.
- Keep your dog sharp and smart and you will have many years of enjoyment with your beloved pet.

TEAK

CHAPTER EIGHT

Harmony in your house.

He is very imprudent, a dog; he never makes it his business to inquire whether you are in the right or the wrong, never asks whether you are rich or poor, silly or wise, sinner or saint. You are his pal. That is enough for him. –
Jerome Klapka Jerome

Imagine reading a book or watching television with your dog lying at your feet chewing on a chew toy. She is relaxed and happy. Or you walk through the house and your dog follows you quietly and calmly. Or you get your dog her food, ask her to sit, put down her bowl and say, "okay" and your dog goes to her food calmly. This is harmony. It's a wonderful thing.

Now imagine your dog barking, running all over the house, knocking down plants or plowing into a wall leaving a hole. You yell at your dog and she runs away making you upset and feeling guilty. This is not harmony this is chaos! How do you get back the harmony and good feeling about having a dog in the house?

Here's how:

- Teach your dog basic obedience.
- Exercise your dog to burn off the unwanted energy.
- Keep your dog on a leash in the house until she learns it is not a place to run.
- Reward your dog when she's quiet.
- Keep your dog's life interesting and fun.
- Become a pack leader and have rules and boundaries.

CHAOS VS HARMONY IN BEBE'S WORLD:

"I live in a house with three boys, one big boy, Brenan and two little boys, Colten and Hayden. The little boys run everywhere, all around the house, up and down the stairs. I run after them. I nip at their legs. I bark. I jump. We play big time wrestling. The big boy likes to wrestle with me. He yanks, pulls me and pins me. I bark and nip at him. This is part of the game. Sometimes I bite. Then I get in trouble. My mistress tells them to stop. No running. No wrestling. But boys will be boys and I like to play with my boys.

When the boys go to school I'm alone with the mistress. I follow her. She doesn't run. She doesn't wrestle. She vacuums. I don't like the vacuum. I run away. She cooks. I stand by the stove and watch her cook. I smell the food. I want some. I beg. She loves me so sometimes she gives me human food. My girlish figure is a little large.

When she works on her computer I lay down by her. She pets me and tells me, "You're a good dog Bebe." My mistress talks on the phone. I watch her talk. I'm company for her.

Then the boys are home from school and its chaos again, running, yelling, jumping. I get frazzled. I sneak into the dark laundry room and fall asleep on the cool tile.

At night when the master comes home I run to greet him. I jump up on his leg. I'm little so I get away with it. When we have dinner I sneak under the table and put my little foot on my mistress's leg. She is my best chance of getting a bite of food.

After the boys are in bed I jump up in my master's lap and watch TV with him. He pets my head and tells me, "I love you Bebe."

COLTEN AND BEBE

CHAPTER NINE

Who your Dog likes and who they don't like!

Dogs are miracles with paws. – Susan Kennedy

We have gone over some of the information in this chapter already. I'm going to write some more about it because when you understand it completely you will have a better relationship with your dog.

If you want a dog to like you:
- Make sure you meet his needs: water, food, shelter and affection.
- Be sure your dog trusts you and the other family members.
- Train your dog.
- Socialize your dog.
- Make his life interesting and fun.
- Express affection with petting, hugs or treats.

- Be a strong leader, have rules and boundaries.

Situations that dogs don't like:

- Don't yell or hit your dog. It will confuse and scare him.
- Suppose someone came up to you speaking in a strange language telling you to do something, you try to figure out what the human wants but you are confused.
- If a dog is frightened or confused he will bark, growl, run away or bite.
- Don't be a weak leader who is mean to get your way, your dog will be frightened and he will not trust you.

Always help your dog understand what you want with a gentle touch, good instruction and a friendly voice. Celebrate with your dog when he does a good job. Your dog will like you and try to please you. Dogs will learn quickly if you are a good leader who is fair, helpful and encouraging.

When you build your dog's self-esteem and confidence he will want to be around you because he likes you.

The same is true of people.

CHAPTER TEN

Hierarchy – What is Pack Mentality?

If you're not the lead dog, the view never changes. Anonymous

Understand pack mentality; it's your dog's nature.

- Our dogs are descended from a small subspecies of wolf.
- His body organs are like the wolf's body organs. They both have 78 chromosomes.
- Dogs and wolves can breed. The dog is called a hybrid.
- A dog's senses, pack instincts and the color of his coat is inherited from the wolf.
- Look for specials on Wolves on the Discovery Channel. It can help you understand your dog's social organization and how they communicate.
- A dog is an animal first and then a pet.
- Do not treat your dog like your child or your baby. It will confuse him.

- If you have more than one dog let them work out who's the boss. The first dog is the alpha dog. The second dog is the subordinate.
- Greet the alpha dog first then the other dogs or you will confuse the dogs and they may fight to establish alpha dog status.
- Once you establish a rule or boundary don't break it. Who wants to follow a leader who can't make up their mind?
- If the fighting becomes too aggressive you should step in to avoid injury to your dogs. Call a dog trainer for advice if you're confused about what steps to take to avoid fighting or to break up a dog fight safely.

What if your parents told you there is no hitting. Then one day you hit your brother and he cries. Your parents see it but don't say anything. Now, you are confused, you just hit your brother and got away with it. So does that mean that when your parents make rules you can break them?

When parents are not leaders it will confuse the children. The same thing is true with the dog. If you are not a good leader it will confuse the dog. There will be a break down in the pack because a dog expects a strong leader and if there isn't one then they will try to become the leader. They will boss you around.

TANK'S STORY:

"Hi everyone! My name is Tank. I'm a puppy French bulldog. I just moved in. All the people who meet me say, "What a cute dog! He's so sweet!" Bebe's mistress likes to take my little face in her hands and say, "Look at that face. I love that little face.""

All the people in my family are very familiar with dog training because my mistress is a dog trainer. They immediately established rules about who the boss is and who the boss isn't. I'll tell you who the boss isn't. Me, that's who.

Right after I moved in my master got a puppy too. Her name is Tommie and she's a Belgain Malinois. She grew bigger than me really fast. Now she's a big, big dog and I'm so small they call me "Teeny Tiny." The people in the family watch us closely. I love to wrestle with Tommie but she's so big she can pin me in a second.

The family wants us to work out our hierarchy. They want us to decide between ourselves who's the pack leader so we can stay friends and not get mad at each other. But they also don't want us to hurt each other.

When Tommie is getting pets I try to muscle in so I get more pets than she does. Tommie is a good girl and she lets me get away with it. Sometimes she tries to take my toy and I growl and snap at her until she leaves it alone. Sometimes the family has to stop our arguments and the toy gets taken away if we continue to fight over it.

The main thing is that I like her and I like to play with her. She likes me too but she doesn't know how big she is and at times I forget that I am small.

The family is very careful about the way they treat us and how we treat each other. We all get along and we all love each other. "It's a happy house to live in."

CHAPTER ELEVEN

Attitude – Dogs can read your vibes.

It is true that whenever a person loves a dog he derives great power from it. – Old Seneca Tribal Chief

Whenever I'm instructing a basic obedience group I pick out the dog who is giving his poor owner the hardest time. Within minutes the dog follows my commands. The owner and group members are blown away as they watch the dog calm down and behave.

I explain to the group the reason why I'm successful training dogs:

- Attitude is everything when training a puppy or dog.
- Establish a top dog attitude.
- Remain assertive and calm while giving commands and your dog will be relaxed.
- Assertive does not mean aggressive.

- Assertive means you firmly ask your dog to do something.
- Your dog is expected to be submissive calm.
- Submissive means your dog will do as you say.
- Be consistent and persistent. Give commands the same way each time and keep at it until your dog obeys you.
- I reward the dog continuously when they obey. I tell them "good dog" or I give them a treat or a pet.
- I'm patient.
- It's important to remember a dog survives by using all their senses. First smell than sight and hearing. Let them smell. It won't hurt you and your dog will learn everything they need to know about you and the people who come to your house.

When training is not as successful:

- When you are sick you are not in the mood to train. Your dog will become restless and not follow through with commands.
- A dog watches you and tries to figure out what you want of them. If you are angry, anxious or have too much energy during training your dog will know it.
- If you try to rush through training, you may get upset because your dog won't follow through with the commands.
- When your energy level is high or your face is strained your dog will sense something is wrong.
- A dog can smell a nervous odor and they can hear a voice that is not in a normal range. Your dog will be nervous if you are nervous.

- Take a break, calm down and training will be more fun and more successful.

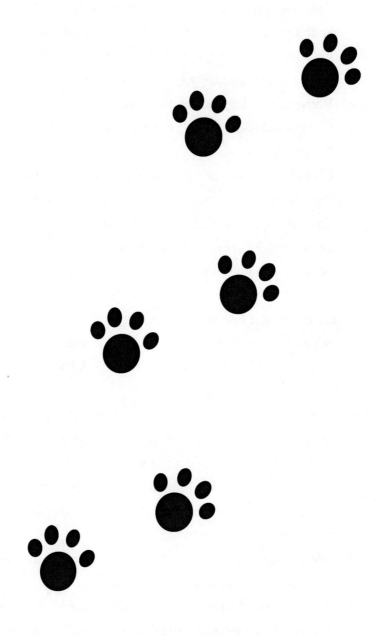

CHAPTER TWELVE

Aggression.

Money will buy you a fine dog, but only love can make it wag its tail. – Richard Friedman

If your dog is aggressive look for a trainer who can help you understand what type of aggressive behavior you are dealing with and how you can treat it.

Aggression:
- Aggression is threats through posturing, barking, growling or staring.
- Aggression can be offensive or defensive. Dogs can chase and bite. They can also bite and run away.
- Sex, age, size, hormonal status, territory, personal distance, the desire to be the alpha dog and some people can cause aggression. The alpha dog is the boss of the pack.
- Think of the things that make you mad. The same things that upset you can upset your dog.

- Dogs are pack animals, they don't expect equality. Their minds are not wired up that way.
- The dog's nature is to find his place in the pack, the dominance hierarchy. Once he finds his place he's fine with it.

What are the different types of dog aggression?

- **Dominance aggression.** One dog fights to become the pack leader.
- **Possessive aggression.** A dog fights for his territory or something that belongs to him like his food, his toys or his owner.
- **Fear aggression.** If a dog is scared he will growl or bite.
- **Protective aggression.** He will protect you if he thinks you are in danger.
- **Inter-male aggression.** He will fight to be the alpha dog.
- **Predatory aggression.** A dog is a hunter by nature.
- You can teach a dog to be aggressive.

Here's how to prevent aggression:

- Don't choose an aggressive breed unless you are willing to learn how to work with aggressive breeds.
- Socialize your puppy as soon as you can. Take him with you when you go out.
- Take him to puppy classes. Many dog trainers have a class that can educate you and your puppy.
- Start basic obedience in a safe environment.
- Socialize by finding a puppy group with healthy puppies.
- Train all the time.

- Make sure your dog can hold a sit/stay and a down/stay without breaking the command. Start with 5 seconds and work up to 15 minutes.
- Stop any threat right away.
- Never let your dog control a walk, growl or bark at anyone or any dog.
- Reward your dog for calm behavior, encourage good behaviors.
- Neuter or spay your dog.
- Keep the dog's daily life exciting and fun.
- Feed your dog after you have eaten.
- Don't pet a dog when he is being mean. It rewards him for being aggressive.
- Be firm with him. "No or Leave it." Use a strong voice.
- Don't play games that encourage aggressive behaviors.
- Never hit your dog.
- Stop aggression the minute you see it or he will become more aggressive until one day he hurts someone.

MAX'S STORY.

Max is a little dog who lived on the streets for a long time. When he finally found his way to Andy, his present owner, he was very aggressive. He was especially aggressive with dogs that were bigger than him.

Andy worked with Max constantly. She used all the Angel Dogs Training techniques until Max was retrained into an adorable, loving, sweet dog.

He came to basic obedience classes to become socialized. He joined "therapy dog" classes to learn how to be calm when anyone came near him.

Max just passed the Angel Dogs Therapy Group. He's a miracle.

CHAPTER THIRTEEN

Games you can play with your dog.

The dog was created especially for children. He is the god of frolic. –
Henry Ward Beecher

Playing games with your puppy can be fun but some games will cause aggression so be careful which games you choose.

Games you should play:
- **Treat Game:** Throw a treat, but not too far. As the puppy runs for the treat back up a little to put some distance between you and him. After the puppy eats the treat ask him to come to you and sit. When he sits give him a treat. This game will teach your dog fetch, come and sit. It will also teach your dog to sit instead of jumping on you. This is important. You don't want your puppy

to jump on you. You want him to come to you, sit and look up at you to see what you want him to do next.

- **Fetch:** Is similar to the Treat Game except you throw a ball or a toy. When your dog gets good at fetch you can teach him to catch a Frisbee or join a flyball group. Throw the ball and tell your dog to "fetch." When your dog gets the ball call him back to you. Say, "come" and give the hand signal for come which is to sweep your hand to your chest with your palm toward you. When the dog brings the ball to you tell him to "sit" and give the hand signal for sit which is to bend your elbow and sweep your hand up to your shoulder with your palm toward you. Ask your dog to drop the ball. Say, "drop." Pick up the ball and throw it again. We'll go over the hand signals once more in a later chapter. A good place to teach your dog to fetch is in a narrow hallway. He has to bring the ball back down the hallway to you. He can't go running off with the ball. Tell him, "good fetch." Not all dogs like to play "fetch" so don't feel sad or upset when your dog does not want to retrieve a ball or toy. Instead find a game your dog does like and have fun!

- **Hide and Seek:** Have someone hold your puppy by her collar while you hide. Find a good hiding place and yell out, "Come and get me." This is the signal for the person who is holding your puppy to let go. When she finds you celebrate and tell her what a good dog she is. Give her a treat. This game will teach your dog to come when you call. If your dog gets good at this game you can join a Track and Field Club that will teach your dog to find special things they hide in bushes or in containers. You can find these clubs on line or ask your trainer.

- **Yo-Yo Game:** Teaches your dog to come to different people. Everyone sis in a circle with the puppy in the center. Someone calls the puppy. When the puppy obeys, give him a big pet or a treat. Then someone else calls the puppy to them and they repeat the greeting. Cheerios are a good training treat.

- **Basic Obedience:** Is a trick game. You teach your dog tricks like sit, stay, come, down and heel. It's fun and rewarding. You want the puppy to do what you ask and learn to follow through with the commands you give him.

Games you should not play:

- **Tug of War:** Don't tug a toy left and right. It will teach a dog to be aggressive. He may grab shirt sleeves, dresses, shoe laces, pant legs, etc. When playing a tug game you pull forward and the dog pulls backward. To end the game let go of the toy or tell the dog to "drop" the toy. You are in charge at all times.

- **Chasing:** Don't teach your dog to chase you. Dogs are predators and when he hunts he chases his prey. He will jump on you and knock you down. He doesn't want to hurt you but this is what a dog will do when he is being a dog. There are breeds that want to herd. When you run the dog will nip at your heels and growl to herd you around. This can be scary because you think your dog is trying to bite you and hurt you. He could hurt you. Choose a safe game when you play with your dog. Your dog can run with you. He can run alongside for exercise but he can't chase you.

- **Big Time Wrestling:** Don't wrestle. Your dog could hurt you. When you wrestle with your dog he will think it's a way to dominate or even hunt you down. Your dog may bite you and then he will get in trouble. This is not a game.

BEBE'S STORY:

"I live with boys. The two little boys let me chase them through the house. They wrestle. They play tug of war. I grab their clothes and they yank and crank all over the place so I'll let go and they can win. They have friends who play the same games with me.

I'm a Jack Russell Terrier and my breed of dog used to keep barns free of small rodents. When I chase the little boys I nip at their legs. It's something I can't help doing.

The other day a little girl came into our backyard. I didn't know her. She ran around screaming. She scared me. I wanted her out of our backyard. I barked and snapped at her.

Grandma ran out of the house and yelled, "Bebe no. Stop that!" I didn't listen. The little girl started to cry. Grandma tried to catch me or chase me away but I'm a quick little dog. I'd run away and then come back from another direction.

Finally Grandma had one of my boys and his friend, take the girl out of the yard. Then I settled down.

My trainer tells the little boys I should not chase them, yank and crank or bark and snap at anyone. All of their friends should know these rules and follow them.

Sometimes I get excited and forget all my training. I bark. I jump up on them. I could do a lot of damage. I could hurt someone big time. Grandma says I'm like the littlest boy who runs around yelling and pinching people to get attention. He thinks he's playing. He needs to learn the right way and the wrong way to play just like me.

Colten is going to take me to agility training. There will be other dogs for me to play with. Small dogs like me and my friend Miller and big dogs like Timber. I can't wait.

AGILITY TRAINING
MILLER

CHAPTER FOURTEEN

No Big Time Wrestling.

A dog wags his tail with his heart. – Martin Buxbaum

There are a few things you should never do when you or your friends play with your dog. I want to go over them once more because they're important.

NEVER EVER:
- Don't wrestle with your dog. Your dog could get hurt or they could bite you.
- Tell your friends not to wrestle with your dog. If your dog bites your friend it will make their parents angry. They may even sue your parents. Your dog's actions are your responsibility. Don't be afraid to tell your friends "no." They will respect you for it.
- Don't let your friends run up to your dog yelling and shouting. It will freak your dog out. He may bark and

snap. It's a natural thing for your dog to do. Tell your friends to be calm around your dog.

- No running in the house. Your dog will chase you. That's not good. The dog will think he's hunting or herding you. He will snap at your legs.
- Don't let your dog chase you. Its one thing when he's a little harmless puppy but puppies can grow into big heavy dogs.
- Don't let your dog race around the house. A big dog can knock your grandmother flat. Then your dog will be in trouble. Keep your dog out of trouble.
- Never, ever hit your dog. Its mean and it doesn't help anything. Be gentle, be calm, and be firm.
- If your dog is sleeping don't run up and jump on him or put your face near his mouth, you can get bit. Always wake your dog by calling his name then wait until he comes to you.
- If your dog is sleeping on the couch don't grab his collar and pull him off, you can get bit.

Some people think you have to teach a dog to protect you. Some even believe you should hit a dog to make him mean so he will protect you. They are wrong. Some dogs will naturally protect you. If someone tries to hurt you your dog could growl, snap or even bite. Be careful when you're playing with your friends. If your dog thinks you're being hurt they might go after your friend to protect you.

Pay close attention to these things. This will make the difference between a sweet loving dog and an aggressive dog. It's the aggressive dogs who find themselves in the pound. We don't want that.

CHAPTER FIFTEEN

Hand Signals and Basic Obedience.

Do not make the mistake of treating your dogs like humans or they will treat you like dogs. – Martha Scott

"Basic Obedience" is the beginning stage of dog training. It takes a dog about 30 days to understand a command completely. Spend at least 10 minutes in the morning and 10 minutes in the evening working on commands. As the weeks progress, add more time to your training sessions.

I begin with heel, then each week I add another command or two. Always say your dog's name first, then the command. "Timber, Heel." Say your dog's name to get her attention.

HEEL:
- Attach a leash to your dog's head collar, harness or flat collar.

- Your hand signal is to slap the side of your left leg which will alert your dog that you want them to heel and it will remind you to start with your left foot. Say, "Timber, Heel."
- Walk your dog at your side with her front feet even with your feet. She can be a little behind you but never in front.
- Walk at your normal pace. If the dog looks around too much and seems to lose interest try walking faster.
- When a dog leads a walk, in her mind, she takes control which means she will lead you where she wants to go, not where you want to go.
- Your dog will drag you from one bush to another or bark at strangers or other dogs.
- Once she knows who is in control she will relax and not be assertive.
- Practice in front of your home.
- Turn left, right, and make 180 degree turns.
- Do "stop and goes," big circles, squares, feel your dog through the leash.
- Keep your leash loose so she will find a spot at your side where she doesn't feel any pressure. If she feels continuous pressure she will begin to struggle with the leash.
- When your dog pulls on the leash go in the opposite direction or stop and ask your dog to sit. After your dog sits walk up to their side than walk on.
- Remember to praise your dog every time they are walking at your side.
- As you add a command, continue to go over the basic commands you've already taught her.

SIT:

- Give the hand signal and ask your dog to "sit." If she does not obey press down on her hindquarters or gently pull up on her head collar until she sits.
- The hand signal is palm toward you while you raise your hand toward your shoulder. Say, "Timber, Sit."
- When she sits reward your dog with a "good sit" and a treat. Use treats for three days only.
- Use a treat to get a dog to sit for you. Show the dog the treat and slowly move the treat backwards towards the dog's ear. When your dog sits give them the treat and say, "Good sit."
- Another option is "luring" with a dog's favorite toy. Use it the same way you would a treat. Reward them with the toy when they complete the exercise.
- Have your dog sit before you go out your front door.
- Slap your left thigh, ask her to heel then step out of the front door first. This will tell her that you are the boss on the walk.
- If she tries to go out the door first, start again. Don't let her go out first.
- When you are on your walk have your dog sit when you cross the street or when you are talking to a neighbor.
- Have her sit when you put on a leash or when you feed her. Demand respect and your dog will have good manners.

STAY:

- Put your dog on a leash so if she tries to walk away and break the command you can correct her instantly.

- There are two hand signals for stay. One is when your dog is at your side in the heel position; you put your palm in front of her face and gently swing your arm back and forth. The other hand signal is when you are in front of your dog. Lift up your hand, palm facing her and say, "Timber. Stay."

- If she keeps coming toward you stop her, take her back to the spot she was sitting and say, "stay." Keep doing this until she stays.

- Stay is the only command you can repeat. By repeating "stay" your dog will focus on you and not other things.

- When she stays reward her with "good dog" and a treat. Use treats for 3 days. After the 3rd day give your dog a treat occasionally. You don't want her to obey for the treat only. You want her to obey because you ask her to.

- When working the stay command you will step out in front of her on your right leg not your left. Remember left leg means heel, right leg means stay.

- Turn and face your dog as you back away.

- Teach her to sit/stay while you answer the door or go out the door.

- Teach her to sit/stay for her food. Put her food down and don't let her go to the food until you release her by saying "okay."

- The sit/stay is important for dogs that jump on people. A dog cannot attack a person or another dog if she is in a sit/stay.

COME:

- There are several ways to teach a dog to come.
- The hand signal is palm toward you and say "Bebe. Come." Your palm is about waist or chest high sweeping the dog toward you.
- You can teach your dog to come by playing Hide and Seek, the Treat game and Yo-Yo. See Chapter 13 for the rules to these games.
- Reward your dog with "good dog" and a treat when she comes.

DOWN:

- Tell your dog "Timber, Sit." Then tell her "Timber, Down."
- The hand signal for down is to point to the ground.
- If you use a treat, first show your dog the treat than put it near her nose, slowly lower the treat between her toes than slowly move the treat forward. At the same time put gentle pressure on her shoulder.
- The best place to practice a down is on a tile floor because it's slippery.
- When the dog obeys say "good down" and give her a treat.
- The best time to start teaching the down command is after a long walk. Your dog will want to lie down on the cool tile.

NO AND LEAVE IT:

- Don't use your dog's name with a negative command. They may become fearful of their name. They don't always understand English. They do understand your tone of voice.

- Look at your negative word as a freeze word. You can stop your dog from running out the door, across the street or picking up something that could be toxic.
- Say your freeze word once "No, stop, or leave it" then make your dog follow through with the command.
- Don't repeat yourself over and over. Your dog will learn to ignore you if you keep repeating yourself.
- If you use your freeze word when your dog is on a leash he will have to follow through.
- No hitting or yelling. Be gentle. Be loving.
- Look hard into your dog's eyes if they are not obeying right away. Once they look into your eyes they will know you mean it and they will obey.

COLLAR CORRECTION:

- Don't yank too hard.
- A collar correction is a quick soft pop not a hard snap that could hurt his neck or throat.
- Use it to make her pay attention to you, not some leaf blowing along the ground.
- If your dog is pulling to the left you gently correct her to the right or turn to the right and start walking away from your dog she will have to catch up.
- If your dog is pulling forward you gently give a backward collar correction or do a 180 degree turn.
- Don't pull your dog upwards. You could hurt his neck.
- If your dog barks for no reason give him a collar correction and say, "No bark. Quiet."

- Reward your dog when they are quiet say, "good dog."
- When your dog goes after something give him a collar correction and say "leave it."
- Remember a collar correction is not to hurt your dog it is used to get their attention and have them focus on you.

TIMBER'S STORY:

"I was freaked out running along a busy street. I didn't know where to go or what to do. I was starving.

Suddenly a car pulled up and a friendly looking woman stepped out. She opened the back door and called to me. I ran as fast as I could go. I jumped into the safety of her car. I was relieved and happy. Could this be? Will she take me home with her? I had wandered around for days looking for food and water. I was lost and scared.

She drove into the driveway of her house. It has a big yard with a swimming pool and lots of orange trees. She called her husband, Phil, from her cell phone to let him know she was bringing home a stray dog. He was waiting for me in the driveway.

When he let me out of the car I jumped up on him. I wanted to see his face. I wanted to see if I knew him.

"No," he said to me, "off." I was so excited and scared that I didn't listen.

The woman got a head collar and put it on me. I calmed down right away. It felt natural like something my mother used to do to me. The woman took me into the back yard and gave me a big bowl of water and a big bowl of food. I gobbled up the food and drank all the water as fast as I could.

I needed a long time to settle down. At night they put me in a safe comfortable crate with a rug, a blanket and a chew toy. The crate was in their bedroom. I'm comforted by their nearness. I hear them and smell them. They are my new family. I was so exhausted that I slept and slept.

The next day my new mistress took me to the veterinarian. First he scanned me for a microchip. I didn't have one. Veterinarian's put microchips in a dog's neck so they can find their owners if they get lost. Dogs are escape artists and sometimes we get away without knowing what we're doing.

The veterinarian checked me all over and gave me some vaccines. I needed to heal from anxiety and starvation. He told my mistress what kind of dog food was best for me. They made more appointments for vaccines and to have me spayed.

My mistress taught me commands right away. "Sit" was my first command because I jumped on people. "Stay" is another command. I have to "sit and stay" while she gets my food. She puts my dish down and says "okay" before I can eat.

They kept me on a training leash. They step on it if they want to stop me from doing anything I shouldn't do. I had so much to see. It's a big house so I explored every corner. They have two cats that are fearful of me and don't want me there. I want to chase them. I'm not allowed to do that.

One day my mistress put the head collar on me. She slapped her hand to her left thigh and said, "Timber. Heel." She held the leash in her right hand in front of her. It was loose. I walked with her on her left side. She was repeating "good girl" in a light and friendly voice. It made me feel good and happy. If I tried to pull away she turned around and went the other way so I had to follow her. She does this to get my attention and to keep me from going where I want to go. The minute I caught up with her I heard that happy friendly voice. Boy, do I love my walks!

My mistress and my master worked on all the commands every day for a few minutes in the morning and a few minutes in the evening. They were firm with me. I didn't jump on them. I obeyed when they told me to do something. Than comes the praise and sometimes a treat reward, yummy!

I'm proud to say that I am now a well behaved dog with good manners. Sometimes I need to be reminded not to push in the door and not to bother the cats but I just can't help myself. It's fun to bother the cats. Besides I want them to know I'm the boss over them.

Everyone loves me. I'm good around children. I would never hurt them. I like to play. I have to be reminded to be careful. Once I jumped on the little boy and knocked him down. My master said, "No," in a firm voice and told me to sit. He made sure the little boy was okay and explained to him that I don't know how big I am and that I don't mean to hurt him. I am not allowed to get away with that kind of behavior. My master apologized to the little boy for me. I don't do that anymore.

My master and my mistress spend a lot of time training me. I'm a good dog and they love me. They're glad they decided to keep me. I've had agility training and I'm a therapy dog. That's pretty good. I went from lost to awesome in a short period of time. "Mostly....I'm happy."

EILEEN AND TIMBER

CHAPTER SIXTEEN

Working with Distractions

As I walk my dog I wonder would I be walking as much without her. – Eileen Tonick

If your dog is fat, you aren't getting enough exercise. – Unkown

Imagine walking in your neighborhood. It's a beautiful day. The wind is breezy. A car goes by and you turn to look at it. You smell beef barbecuing. It makes your mouth water. You hear children in the distance laughing and calling to one another. You turn to watch them. Your friend walks up to you and touches your shoulder. All of these noises, smells, sights and touches are distractions. The same is true for dogs. They are distracted by smells, sights, sounds or touch. You can train your dog to focus and ignore distractions.

How to work with distractions:
- Join a basic obedience group. Working with other people and dogs will give you a great start.

- Teach your dog the "leave it" command to prevent her from smelling bushes, chasing bunnies or picking up things.
- Practice passing another dog without your dog losing control.
- Be in charge of your daily walks. Don't let your dog make you do what she wants to do.
- Remember, you are assertive calm and your dog is submissive calm. That means you calmly control the situation and your dog calmly submits to your commands.
- Control your energy level. Keep your energy low. Stay neutral.
- Socialize your dog every day until their surrounding becomes so familiar they won't act out.

TIMBER'S DISTRACTIONS:

"I'm a curious dog. I want to explore. I want to see it. I want to smell it. When my mistress takes me for a walk in a new place I can hardly contain myself.

"Look, look. Isn't that odd? What is that?" I pull on my leash. "Let's go see that. I want to smell that." If we see a new person that I don't know I pull on the leash, "Let's go say hi."

My mistress takes me for a walk in the neighborhood everyday. It's good exercise for me and her. We walk all over the neighborhood. At first it was exciting and frightening. It's not so strange or scary anymore.

If we see a neighbor my mistress makes me sit. That way I can't jump on them. I want the neighbor to pet me but some people don't like dogs. Some people are allergic to dogs.

I love kids. I want to play with them. My mistress says, "Leave it," and sometimes she has to pop my leash. This reminds me we're on a walk and I should pay attention to her.

I love to smell bushes. I want to know which dogs were there before me. Maybe they peed on the bush. I strain on my leash I hear, "Leave it." I turn my attention back to my mistress she tells me, "Good dog." The first time we went on walks she had treats in her pocket. When she corrected me and I did what she wanted she would give me a treat. That let me know I was doing the right thing. After a couple of days she stopped giving me the treats but she still expected me to obey commands.

CHAPTER SEVENTEEN

Behavior.

A boy can learn a lot from a dog: obedience, loyalty and the importance of turning around three times before lying down.
– Robert Charles Benchley

A dog owner gets rid of their dog because of behavioral problems. In this chapter we're going to learn what they are and deal with them effectively. All problems can be solved with rules, boundaries and basic obedience.

Mouthing:
- It's not biting. Biting is painful bruising or breaking the skin so it bleeds.
- Mouthing is how a puppy learns to use his mouth safely.
- Teach him how much he can mouth without hurting you.
- When your puppy starts to mouth too hard say, "Ouch, no bite." Loudly. When he stops say, "Good dog."

- Puppies mouth when they're frustrated or in pain because teeth are coming in.
- Exercise is a great way to relieve frustrated puppies.
- Ice cubes, chewies, cold carrots can relieve a sore mouth.
- Dogs like cold carrots. They also like apples but be sure and cut the seeds out. The seeds are bad for them.

Jumping:
- Jumping is annoying and dangerous. A dog can knock someone over, hurt or scratch them.
- In a dog's mind jumping is a way to be the boss.
- They jump when they are excited or want to play.
- Pups jump to teach each other how to act like a hunter.
- Dogs jump to let other dogs know they are the leader.

Stop the jumping:
- Ask your dog to sit when they jump.
- Give your dog a treat or a pet when they sit.
- You must show them you are the boss.
- Attach a leash to your dog's collar, than step on the leash so he can't jump.
- For smaller dogs put a chair near the entry door and teach them to sit in the chair while you answer the door.
- Use a squirt bottle to stop your dog from jumping.
- Don't push your dog away with your hands; they may think you want to play.
- Play the fetch, come, sit, treat game.

Barking:

- It's a normal and natural form of communication.
- Barking warns people or other dogs not to come any closer.
- Dogs bark to tell their owner that someone is at the door or near their territory.
- Puppies bark for food, warmth, or when they are hurt or frustrated.
- They bark when they chase something or someone in fun.
- Play barking is high pitched and happy.
- Aggressive barks are low pitched and growling.
- Some dogs bark at a certain time of day, like morning, much like a rooster crows.
- Dogs will bark when they are excited or lonely.

Stop the barking:

- Teach your dog to bark on command. Say, "Bark, Whoff." Keep repeating until your dog whoffs then give them a treat. The end result is you say bark and your dog barks. Remember to practice every day for 2 to 5 minutes.
- Once you teach them to bark on command teach them to be quiet.
- When your dog barks say, "Quiet, no bark." When they are quiet say, "Good quiet," and give them a treat.
- Remember to slowly stop using treats after the third day.
- If your dog barks and disturbs your neighbors when you are not home, use a Citronella anti-bark collar.
- Give your dog lots of exercise and basic obedience.

- If your dog barks because he's lonely take him to a puppy day care center while you're gone.
- Have someone stop by and take him for a walk.
- Leave the TV or the radio on.

Chewing:

- Bored dogs have too much energy and chewing calms them.
- It's a way to relieve pain in their mouth due to new teeth.
- It keeps teeth clean.

Stop destructive chewing:

- Exercise your dog twice a day.
- Give him lots of chew toys.
- Don't leave things around that you don't want him to chew. Doggie proof the house.
- Crate him with his favorite chew toy.
- Make sure his mouth is healthy.
- Take your dog to a day care center if he is home alone.
- Have a dog walker come to your home and exercise your dog.
- Take your dog to work with you if you can.
- Make his life exciting and fun. Join an agility or flyball group.
- Teach him to pull you on your skate board.
- Spray the places your dog chews with bitter apple or vinegar water.
- **Digging:**

- Dogs root out prey, like gofers, that are underground. If you see him digging away like a maniac that may be what he's doing.
- He buries toys or bones so he can find them later.
- Excess energy makes a dog restless. Digging relieves that.
- Separation anxiety causes him to be anxious because you are not there. He may dig to calm himself.
- He has barrier frustrations. He wants to run around outside. He can see, hear or smell things on the other side of the fence.
- We teach him to dig by gardening. He starts to mimic you.
- If it's a hot day a dog will dig to find cooler ground.

Ways to stop digging:
- Provide an area where the dog can dig.
- Remove prey that lives underground.
- Exercise your dog daily and practice basic obedience.
- Booby-trap the areas where your dog digs. Spread chicken wire under the ground.
- Use an outdoor kennel.
- Watch your dog from inside the house, leave a window open, the minute he starts to dig yell, "Leave it." When he stops digging tell him "Good dog."

Housebreaking:
- Crate train your puppy. Dogs usually will not pee where they sleep. Leave him in the crate at night. When you

take him out, take him directly to the place he is allowed to pee.

- Keep him on a leash with you. You wouldn't let a baby wander all over the house.

- Take your puppy to the same area to pee each time. The odor will build and stimulate your puppy to go potty.

- Use a key word whenever your puppy starts to pee. I like to use "do your business" because if there are children in the house parents will yell out, "Did you go potty?" The dog will think that means him and he will stop and go potty.

- Feed your puppy breakfast, lunch and dinner, not all day.

- Put up the drinking water after 6 p.m. If your puppy is thirsty give him a little water.

- A puppy can't control his bladder. Take him to potty every hour for the first month. One month, one hour, then at two months take him every two hours.

- Most puppies have bladder control by 6 months.

- If your puppy goes potty in the house frequently. Make sure he doesn't have a bladder infection or worms.

- Go out the same door every time to establish a routine.

MIGHTY MAX:

"Hello. My name is Max. I'm a two year old Lhasa Apso. I'm cute. I'm tiny. I wandered the streets for a long time before I was found by a nice woman. She took me in and tried to find my owner.

She fed me. She made an appointment with a groomer. The groomer shaved me down to my skin to get rid of all the mattes and the bugs.

She couldn't keep me so she introduced me to one of her neighbors, Andy. Andy is a nice lady but I didn't trust anyone. I barked. I especially barked if other dogs came near me. While I lived on the streets dogs chased me and tried to hurt me. I attacked them to protect myself. I growled and barked and charged them to make them run away.

The woman who saved me decided I should go to the Humane Society because she couldn't control me. Andy said, "No. Don't do that. Let me see if I can work with him." I went to live with Andy and her husband. I was a pain in the butt. A big pain in the butt.

Andy's other friend Cher said, "Bring Max to this Basic Obedience class I'm taking." Cher took her dog and Andy took me to Angel Dogs Training. The trainer Eileen watched me do my thing. Fighting the leash. Barking. Trying to attack the other dogs.

Andy asked, "Is this hopeless?"

"No. Not at all," said Eileen. "This is a great little dog. We'll have him right in no time."

Eileen put a head collar on me. I was taught a command each week. Andy walked me and trained me every day. I wore the head collar all day. When I barked I got a correction and a "Quiet. No Bark." If I tried to attack another dog I got a collar correction and "Leave it." When I was good I got lots of praise and sometimes a treat.

The veterinarian told Andy I am in good health and that I am a good dog. I finally calmed down. I felt safe with Andy. I did well in my classes. I didn't fight the leash, bark and attack.

That was six months ago. Since then I've learned how to be a therapy dog. My trainer says I will be a good therapy dog. The patients will love me because I'm so little and cute.

I am happy to say that Andy and I passed our test and we are now a therapy team.

MAX
THERAPY DOG

CHAPTER EIGHTEEN

Affection

A dog is the only thing on earth that loves you more than you love yourself. – Josh Billings

Affection is a big thing for dogs and humans. But dogs see affection and reward in everything you do for them.

It can be as simple as:
- Water.
- Food.
- Treats.
- Walks.
- A game of fetch.
- A safe warm place to live with a comfortable bed.
- A soft friendly voice.

You don't have to pet your dog to show affection:

- Petting can cause a problem if you pet at the wrong time.
- If your dog barks and you pet her to make her stop, you reward her. It tells her it is good to bark.
- If you pet her when she's anxious you're telling her it's good to be nervous. You can create separation anxiety. She will be nervous and upset every time you leave.
- If your dog makes you pet her she is the boss.
- Don't pet your dog every time she wants it. Pet her when you want to pet her.
- Save the petting for the end of the day when you are hanging out and you are both relaxed. That rewards your dog for calm behavior.

TIMBER, THE AFFECTIONATE DOG:

"I'm a needy dog. I want to be petted all the time. I don't care if you're working. I don't care if you're talking on the phone or if you're on the computer. I want petting. I don't care if you're watching TV. I'll come and lay my head in your lap and wait. I'll go and get my ball and give it to you. Play, play, pet, pet.

My mistress wants to break me of this needy habit because if you pet me anytime I want I will believe I'm the boss. She tells me I'm not.

I like it when the little boys come over to swim. I can always get them to pet me. My mistress watches me. If I get to be a pest she corrects my bad manners. She never gives up. She's like the pet police.

HAYDEN AND TIMBER

CHAPTER NINETEEN

Training the people you live with how to care for your dog.

My dog can make me do all kinds of tricks for her, throw a ball, open and close a door, roll on the floor. Eileen Tonick

Hey kids! When you bring a puppy or a dog into your home it's a big responsibility for all the people who live there.

Involve the family:
- Everyone should train and raise the dog.
- Give proper hand signals.
- Use the right commands.
- Know and practice the solution to a behavioral problem.

When you train together you will also bond with your family. Take your mother or father with you when you walk your dog. That way you can spend some quality time with your parents and help them train the family dog. Make it fun.

When you bring a puppy or dog into your home:

- Take a basic obedience class together or have a trainer come to your house.
- Have someone feed the dog; someone clean up the poop and someone walk the dog.
- Share the grooming chores.
- Make a weekly chart so everyone knows what they have to do that week with the dog.
- Take the dog on outings with the family.
- Play with your dog.
- Do not make it one person's job, make it a family effort. Then no one will complain because they always have to take care of the dog.
- Mom should not be the only person taking care of the dog. She already has enough to do.
- Have fun. Include him when you play with your friends.
- You want to have a family companion that is a joy to be around.
- Do the best you can. Do what's right. Work on it. Keep refining it every day.

BEBE'S FAMILY

"I have a big family who loves me. Everyone takes care of me. I like them all the same.

I was a year old when they got me so I already knew some stuff. I still have some things to learn. My people have some things to learn too.

The boy, Colten, has to pick up my poop. He hates doing that. I don't make big poops so I don't get it. The mistress tells Colten every day that I need a half cup of dog food in the morning and a half cup at night. He's starting to get the idea.

My master tells my mistress not to feed me anything extra. She loves to give me snacks and treats. It makes her feel good because I'm crazy for food.

Jack Russell Terriers are excitable little dogs and I'm no exception. I heard a man tell my master one day, "I had one of those Jack Russell Terrorists."

When Grandma comes to visit I'm so excited to see her that I pee on the floor. Then I walk in it and jump up on her. She is helping me learn not to jump and to hold my pee.

At night I sleep under my master's side of the big huge bed. He doesn't mind because he likes me. He even put a little rug under the bed for me to sleep on. I like being close to him and the mistress. I collect things and store them under the bed. I have a DVD cover, a plastic dinosaur, a sock, a plastic car and one of my chew toys under there. The whole under the bed is my bedroom. It even has a bed ruffle that hangs down all around to give me privacy.

I love to take a shower with the master. Every time he goes into his bathroom I run in and jump on the shower door. My friend Timber doesn't like water but I love water. Give me a good shower. My master thinks this is funny so he lets me take a shower with him. He soaps me up all over and gives me a good rinsing. I'm a clean little dog.

The big boy likes to wrestle with me. He likes to hear me growl. I chew on him a little. Not big bites. Little bites. Our trainer doesn't like this behavior. "Please don't do that," she says, "Bebe will think its okay to growl and snap at people. It is not okay!"

Because I'm so little I'm allowed to get up on the furniture. I love to curl up on the cool leather couch and take a nap. Sometimes the littlest boy will fall asleep on the couch and I try to jump up next to him. If Grandma is there she says, "Bebe!" I know immediately that I can't go up there because I will wake him up. He can be cranky when he's tired and everyone wants him to have his "beauty sleep" in the afternoon.

I don't go on long walks as often as I would like. Everyone is busy and during the summer it's hot in Arizona. I like to go on walks in the neighborhood. I know all the kids because they come to the house. I'm constantly trying to sneak out. There's always a pile up at the door with kids trying to get in or out without letting me out. But I'm fast so I squeeze through. Then they have to chase me all over the neighborhood. It's fun. Uh oh. It's my master using his low, no nonsense voice, "Bebe. Come." Then he calls out, "Cookie!" I go. Fast. I jump over the rocks and sprint up the walkway for my cookie.

I get lots of attention from my family. They take me on camping trips. The master tells everyone that I'm the best behaved one.

Colten is going to do an agility class with me because I'm quick. I will love that. I can't wait. Let's go today. Let's go now. Call the trainer.

CHAPTER TWENTY

What does your dog do when you're not there?

A dog is for life, and not just for Christmas. – Slogan of the National Canine Defense League

My life is full. I run a dog training business, work out at a gym, ride my horse, garden, read, cook, clean, visit family and friends. I can't wait to go to bed at night. I'm tired.

I don't sit in the backyard with nothing to do or sit in my home alone for hours each day. I'd go crazy! I'd be bored, unhappy and act out. I would be restless and destructive. What would you choose? What would your dog choose? Everyone would choose a busy life!

We've learned a lot about what to do with your dog. But now you have to go to work or school.

What does your dog do when you're not there?
- If you exercise her a lot, she's tired, you wore her out! She is happy to sleep and take it easy when you are gone.

- If she has a basket full of toys she will play.
- Give your dog a kong. A kong is a hard rubber toy that you can stuff with peanut butter or cheese whiz. That will keep her busy for hours.
- If there are other animals in the house she will hang out with them.
- Leave the TV or the radio on for extra company.

If your dog doesn't have a full life:
- She'll become destructive when you leave.
- That means chewing on your toys and shoes, going potty in the house, or barking for hours.
- If your dog is outside she will dig up your yard, pull up the sprinklers, dig up your plants, or try to escape to look for you.
- Your dog does not know that her behavior is bad. She's lonely, bored and has energy that she needs to burn off.
- Remember, dogs live in the moment and if you yell at her when she's happy to see you she'll get confused.
- You have to correct your dog's behavior the second you see her do it. You can not punish her for something she did an hour ago. She won't understand.
- She'll run away to another part of the house or backyard, she will cower, pee, or growl in fear.
- A few days of this and you'll want to get rid of your dog.

BEBE'S FRIEND:

"I have a friend who lives on my block. His name is Roscoe. His family leaves in the morning and they don't come back until night time. Roscoe is alone in the back yard every day. I can hear him bark.

He's calling out to his family.

One day I heard his master yell at him. Roscoe had torn up the sprinklers in the backyard. It's not the first time I've heard someone yell at Roscoe. It makes me sad because I like Roscoe. He's a cool dude.

I see him sometimes when I'm out for a walk with one of my little boys or when I pull Colten on his skateboard. Roscoe was really excited to see me. He pulled on his leash so he could come over and talk to me. His master didn't want him to come see me. He yelled at Roscoe and yanked on his collar. He took him back to the house. The master thought Roscoe was too hard to walk. It wasn't fun for either of them.

I haven't seen or heard Roscoe lately. I think the family gave him away. I hope someone with more time got him.

CHAPTER TWENTY ONE

Learning how to understand dog body language

Dogs laugh, but they laugh with their tails. – Max Eastman

I learned about dogs by watching them in action at home and during special events. I go to dog shows, agility shows, and police dog competitions. I read books. I hired a trainer to teach me about dog body language. I volunteered as a puppy raiser for Guide Dogs for the Blind.

Watch your dog:
- Look at a dog's face. Is it relaxed? Are the ears forward or back?
- Are the eyes soft or hard? Are the lips relaxed or curled up?
- Go to the front of the dog's body. Is it relaxed or is the dog leaning forward up over its toes?
- In the shoulder area is the hair down or up?

- Towards the rear end is your dog relaxed or leaning forward?
- Is the tail relaxed, stiff or tucked under his belly?
- Is your dog moving in a happy way or is he stiff or shaking?
- Is the dog's hair falling out because he's stressed?
- Is your dog breathing normally or panting?
- Is saliva forming around the mouth?

You want a relaxed dog. Start with the face and work down to the tail.

- Your dog's face is relaxed.
- His eyes are soft.
- His mouth is closed or slightly open for breathing.
- The hair is down from your dog's head to his tail.
- Your dog's tail is relaxed or moving back and forth.
- Your dog is happy and not stressed.
- Some dogs may even make little happy noises.

TIMBER'S ATTITUDE:

"Hi, it's me Timber. I am happy most of the time except when I get into trouble for chasing the cats. Those darn cats! I love them but it is so much fun to watch them run.

One of my favorite times with my owner is when I play ball with her. I love catching the ball in mid air or chasing it. I bring the ball back and she throws it again. I love running and jumping and having fun. My whole body is happy, my face is relaxed, my ears are forward, my eyes are alert and my tail is joyfully dancing around.

My owner laughs when she watches me catch the ball. I can tell she is happy because she looks like me except she does not have a tail to wag back and forth. Poor thing she does not know what she is missing."

TIMBER

CHAPTER TWENTY TWO

Advanced Training – Agility, Flyball.

If you think dogs can't count, try putting three dog biscuits in your pocket and then giving Fido only two of them. – Phil Pastoret

After your dog learns games and basic obedience teach your dog higher levels of play that is fun for the both of you. Dogs like agility training and fly ball. I teach agility classes. Many of the people who take my "one on one" basic obedience or group classes join this class.

I'm not going to spend a lot of time on this subject because this book is about the basics. There are good books and internet sites if you want to know more. Many cities have dog shows that include flyball and agility. Go and watch these dogs. You'll enjoy it. Take your dog with you. It's amazing to watch the owners and the dogs race through the courses together. Dogs of all breeds or mixed breeds are welcome in these sports.

AGILITY:

Why it's good:

- It's another way to bond with your dog.
- The both of you will have a great time.
- It's mentally stimulating.
- You have to run the course too so its good exercise.
- Your dog learns how to be agile, quick and have good balance.
- You and your dog will make friends with others in the group. It's a great way to socialize your dog.

Information about it:

- The object of agility training is to send your dog through an obstacle course….fast!
- The course is a series of ramps, poles, jumps, tunnels, tables and hoops.
- Buy agility equipment or build it. There are great books on building your own equipment.
- Purchase equipment on line or through magazines.
- Join a club or make your own course in your backyard.
- Two national agility organizations have websites you can visit: www.usdaa.com and www.akc.org
- Each group has its own set of rules so make sure it fits your idea about how a group should be taught.
- Payments for these clubs or groups are set up in package plans. You pay a certain amount of money for a number of classes.
- During the first class the instructor passes out paperwork on the rules and regulations of the group and the commands you will learn.

- The instructor takes the group around the course and explains the obstacles and what they're called.
- Your dog will be on leash until he learns how to go through the course and not be distracted by the other dogs.
- When you and your dog get good at racing through the course the instructor will time you and count the faults. A fault is if your dog knocks down a jump or refuses to do something you ask of her.
- Just like any athlete, dogs will have their good days and bad days. The main goal of agility is having fun with your dog.
- Contact a trainer to find out if they teach classes in agility. If they do the trainer will show you how to build a course.

FLYBALL:
- The dog runs down a course and jumps over hurdles.
- He reaches a box at the end of the course.
- He jumps on the box and releases a ball into the air.
- The dog snatches the ball out of the air.
- He races back down the lane jumping over hurdles until he reaches the end.
- The first dog to race through the course and back to the end wins.
- Sometimes you will have relay teams.

There are a number of organizations that set up Fly Ball competitions:
- They welcome new comers.

- They help train your dog.
- Investigate this sport further by reading books.
- Suggestion: Flyball Racing: The Dog Sport for Everyone by Lonnie Olson or Let's Play Flyball by Cathy Consla and Coleen Mrakovich.
- Visit this website: www.insideflyball.com
- There are several Flyball Organizations like: North American Flyball Association (NAFA) www.flyball.org or United Flyball League International (U-FLI) www.u-fli.com

AGILITY TRAINING – IAM

CHAPTER TWENTY THREE

Community Service – Hospital Visits.

He is your friend, your partner, your defender, your dog. You are his life, his love, his leader. He will be yours, faithful and true, to the last beat of his heart. You owe it to him to be worthy of such devotion. - Unknown

After you finish your basic obedience training you can become a "Pet Partner Team." You and your dog will work together to bring joy and health to people who live in a facility where they don't allow pets.

Children with adult supervision can do this. First you become certified by an organization like the Delta Society. You pass a test given by an evaluator that recommends you and your dog as a team. Once you pass this test and become qualified you can take your dog to a center and let people play with your dog. This simple act can brighten a person's day.

How to become a Pet Partner Team:

- Decide what organization you want to be with. Find one through an internet search or ask your veterinarian or your trainer. Sometimes a trainer is also an evaluator.
- Contact them and find out their requirements.
- Pass the written and skills part of the test.
- Find a facility you want to work with and contact the supervisor.
- Make arrangements for weekly visits.

TIMBER'S STORY:

"Sometimes I'm called Tim. My mistress calls me Rabbit Butt. I won't tell you why but she thinks it's funny. I'm a female German Shepherd. My mistress is the dog trainer who is writing this book.

My mistress saw me running along a road three years ago. I was lost and scared. She was afraid I would be hit by a car or truck so she jumped out of her blue jeep, held the door open and called to me. I leaped in her car. I was skinny and dirty. She took me to a groomer where it took two washings to get rid of all the dirt. Later she took me to the veterinarian and had me examined and spayed. She fed me, loved me and hugged me. I adore her. She saved me.

Everyone says I'm a good looking dog now. I'm slim. I have lots of energy. Clear eyes. A damp nose. I like to lick people and rub up against them. My mistress thinks I'm needy. She doesn't always pet me when I want to be petted because she decides when I should be petted. She's the boss. Not me. Boo-Hoo.

I went through some interesting training to be a community pet therapy dog. I liked doing the training. It's good for me to be mentally stimulated.

My mistress took me to a park where there were other dogs. We learned how to be submissive calm and to do the basic behaviors. If my mistress tells me to sit or just gives the hand signal to sit. I sit.

The reason for my training is because my mistress wants to take me to a place where they have children in crisis. I love children. There are nephews in my family. They come to my house to swim. I don't like to swim but I love to run around the pool while they splash me. I like to try and catch the splash in my mouth. The littlest nephew likes to scratch and pet my belly. I love that so much. I can't even tell you.

When we go to see children in crisis I have to be calm so I don't scare them. They have to be calm so they don't scare me. They pet me and hug me.

One little girl is scared of dogs. And I'm kind of big so I scared her a lot. My mistress asked me to sit, which I did. I waited. The little girl watched while the other children touched me and fed me some treats. I waited. I watched her. I wanted her to come to me.

Finally she walked toward me. I was calm. Sitting there. Waiting. Watching. She reached out and touched my nose. I licked her hand. That made her laugh. My mistress gave her a treat to give me. She showed the little girl how to close her hand around my treat. Then she held the treat under my nose so I could smell it. She slowly opened her hand and I licked the treat from her palm. She giggled and asked if she could give me another treat. That made me like this little girl even more.

We go to the children's crisis center as volunteers twice a week. The little girl waits for me. She sits by the door and waits. When I come through the door she smiles. She runs to me and hugs me around my neck. We're friends for life.

CHAPTER TWENTY FOUR

How to pick a trainer.

There's a saying that goes, "You can't teach an old dog new tricks." I don't know who said that first. Was it Benjamin Franklin? Maybe. Whoever it was didn't have it right. You can teach any dog new tricks. It just takes time and patience. - Eileen Tonick

How do you choose a good trainer? How do you find an accomplished trainer that knows dogs and knows all the latest training methods?

Here are some suggestions:
- Ask your veterinarian or friends for a recommendation.
- Go on line and do a search for trainers in your area.
- Interview each trainer and ask specific questions about their training techniques. Where did they get their training? What methods do they follow? How long have they been a trainer?
- Get references from the trainer's previous clients.
- Ask if you can come to one of their training sessions.

- What associations does the trainer belong to.
- Call the Better Business Bureau in your city for a reference.
- Read books on training.
- Check out the local Park and Recreations in your community for dog classes.
- Interview several trainers before you make up your mind.
- Make sure you like your trainer and you can communicate freely with them.
- When choosing how much money to spend on training, don't go with the cheapest.
- Go with the trainer that has a good reputation.
- The object is to have you and your dog trained the right way. You want good results the first time.

BASIC OBEDIENCE LESSONS AND SCHEDULE: BRINGING IT ALL TOGETHER.

Set up a schedule to train your dog. Some of the information was already covered in the book. Use this part separately to work out your training lessons and schedule.

What you want to accomplish:
- Your dog should know all the hand signals and commands.
- He must have good house manners and be socialized.
- You can do this in five weeks or less if you are consistent, patient and calm.

Following are some training tips.
- When you give a command, say your dog's name first to get his attention, "Jake. Sit."
- Don't repeat and repeat a command. It's confusing.
- Let your dog complete the first command before you give a second command.
- Keep your energy low and calm.

- Praise your dog when he completes a command.
- Release your dog from a command with "OK" or "Free."
- Give a command clearly and with confidence. Don't yell.
- Train your dog to complete a command in 3 seconds.
- Correct your dog only if you catch him in the act of doing something inappropriate. Dogs do not understand that they did something wrong an hour ago.
- Be sure that hand and voice signals match.

HEEL COMMAND
(First Week)

"Heel" is a command that has your puppy walk on your left side slightly ahead of your left heel. Their shoulder and front feet should be even with your feet.

- Practice "heel" exercises in your driveway, back patio or a safe quiet location.
- Practice two ten minute sessions each day, one in the morning and one in the evening.
- Start with five right turn squares, then five left turn squares. Next do 180 degree turns, stop and go and circles.
- These exercises will teach you proper leash control, how to use your body to control your dog, verbal and hand signal.
- Walk your dog on a leash in the house. Practice 180 turns in the hallways.
- If you want to practice more than twice daily rest at least 4 hours in between sessions. Include play time.

- Keep a loose leash so you can give proper leash and collar corrections if he tries to pull or his attention wanders.

- Hold the leash in your right hand, leaving your left hand free for collar corrections. Put your thumb through the leash loop and lay the rest of the leash over your first finger.

- Give your dog the command to Heel by saying: "Bebe. Heel." The correct hand signal is a hand slap to the left thigh.

- Start walking with your left foot.

- Change directions each time your dog gets ahead of you.

- Praise your dog each time he responds to the change of direction.

- Ask your dog to sit each time he pulls ahead. Start practicing this skill after you've mastered the sit command.

- Talk to your dog. The sound of your gentle voice is reassuring.

- Keep at it. He'll get it and soon you will be walking down the street like two buddies.

COLTEN AND TIMBER

SIT COMMAND
(Second Week)

"Sit" is the command for your puppy to place his rear haunches on the ground.

TIPS:

- Work your dog twice a day for ten minutes.
- If the floor is slippery put down a rug for her to sit on.
- Find three different routes when you train your dog. Your walk will be more interesting.
- Before crossing the street put your dog in a sit, look both ways, then cross the street. Do this exercise whether a car is coming or not.
- If your dog pulls hard on the leash ask him to sit.

- Before you go in the house ask your dog to sit. You step in first.
- Ask her to sit when you feed her. Place the dish on the floor say, "Timber. Okay," giving her permission to break the sit command.
- The hand signal is to raise your left hand, to your shoulder, palm facing you.
- Praise her by saying, "Good sit."
- If your dog does not sit, gently pull up on her collar and give a gentle push on the rear end as you say "sit."
- Put a treat near the dog's nose, slowly move it between your dog's eyes. When he sits give him the reward.
- Practice at least five sits with each session.
- Your dog will begin to sit automatically.

EILEEN, TOMMIE AND TANK

STAY COMMAND
(Third Week)

"Stay" is a command that makes your puppy stay in one spot and position until you release her.

TIPS:

- Take your time when you teach your dog to stay, do not rush.
- Hold the leash while you practice.
- Ask your dog to sit/stay for his food then release him with "Tank. Okay."
- Ask your dog to sit/stay before you cross a street or when you talk to someone.
- In the house ask your dog to sit/stay when you introduce him to a houseguest.
- After your dog learns on a 6 foot leash, go to a 15 or 30 foot leash.
- Ask your dog to sit/stay when you open a door to the outside.
- When you put your dog in a car ask him to sit/stay than give the command to load up.
- When you take your dog out of a car ask him to stay while you open the door and put on the leash.

Hand signals:

- Extend your left hand in a stop fashion. Palm toward your dog.
- After a few days widen the distance between you and your dog. By the fourth day, jingle the leash as a distraction.
- Walk around your dog while he sits.

- Praise him if he doesn't move.
- Do not stay your dog for long. Increase the time gradually.

From the heel position:
- Place your dog in a sit on your left side.
- Give your dog the command to stay, using both hand and voice.
- The hand signal for stay is left palm toward your dog swinging your arm gently back and forth like a windshield wiper.
- If your dog moves, correct her by gently pulling up on her collar with the leash and slowly relaxing the tension as she relaxes.
- With your right foot, swing in front of your dog so you are facing her.

EILEEN AND TANK

EILEEN AND TOMMIE

COME COMMAND
(Fourth Week)

"Come" requires your puppy to come close enough to let you gently grasp her collar.

TIPS:

- You can teach your dog with games: Yo-Yo, Hide and Seek and On Leash Training Methods.
- Your training session was 10 minutes in the morning and 10 minutes in the evening. Now training time is broken down into 5 to 10 minutes inside the house and 20 to 30 minutes on your walk.
- Practice loose leash training in the house and on your walk.

- Do at least 7 successful sit/stay and 3 come exercises.
- Use the proper voice and hand signals.
- Do not get tense or anxious.
- Do not ask your dog to "come" if it's for something you know they don't like. Example: nail clipping. Gently go and get them, put them on a leash and then clip their nails.
- From a sit position, ask your dog to stay.
- Walk out to the end of the leash. Pause for a moment say, "Timber. Come." The hand signal is to sweep your open hand, palm toward your waist or chest area.
- If needed give a slight leash correction towards you.
- Make sure she stops in front of you and ask her to sit.
- As your dog looks up at you, praise her, "Good. Timber."

OFF LEASH

- Practice in a controlled environment such as your house or a fenced backyard.
- Use a calm friendly voice.
- Praise your dog for coming to you even if you are correcting her.
- Do not repeat the command "come" hoping for a response.
- If you are in an enclosed fenced area walk or run backwards to have the dog follow you.
- Use treat, toys or make funny noises to get your dog's attention.

EILEEN AND TIMBER

YO-YO GAME

- Have 2 or more people sit or stand six feet apart. Have the two people take turns calling your dog and giving her a treat.
- Everyone should use the same words "Bebe. Come." Use a happy voice.
- As your dog learns to come, increase the distance.
- Give her a treat when she comes. Cheerios are good.
- Put your hand on her collar before you give the treat.
- Gradually increase the distance.
- Gradually increase the distractions.

HIDE AND SEEK GAME

This is a fun way to teach your dog to come to you. Kids love this. Have someone gently hold your dog in one room of the house. Hide in another room. Your first hiding places should be very easy. Make it easy for your dog to succeed. Call her, "Bebe. Come." When she finds you welcome her warmly. Put your hand on her collar and give her a treat.

Children should not run away from the dog. As an added safe guard for small children, teach your dog to sit before the child gives her a treat. Start hiding in more difficult places further away. Next, go outside and play the game in a safe, enclosed environment.

DOWN COMMAND
(Fifth Week)

"Down" is a command to get your puppy to lie down on the ground.

TIPS:
- The down command is hard for some dogs because they have to submit more than they want to.
- Practice 5 down/stays each training session.
- Ask your dog to do a down/stay for his meals.
- Start with a five second down and then increase the time.
- By your 3rd week your goal will be a 5 minute down/stay in the house. Your goal is a 15 minute down/stay.
- Practice down/stays while you watch TV or while you eat.
- Have a special place, like a doggy bed, where he can practice a down/stay.

- If your dog is nervous about doing a down/stay outside, practice in the house for 3 days, then go to your backyard. After that do down/stay on your walks.
- When your dog is lying around tell her, "Good down." This will get her familiar with the word.
- Praise your dog for a good job.
- Make sure the area is not ant infested and that the ground is not hot or too cold.
- Place your dog on your left side in the sit position.
- Give the command, "Bebe. Down," use the correct verbal and hand signal.
- The hand signal is to point to the ground.
- Go down on one knee and say, "down" again using the hand signal.
- If your dog doesn't go down put your arm across her shoulders and walk her feet out slowly into the down position.
- Use a treat reward or lure. Hold the treat or lure firmly, move your hand slowly straight down between your dog's feet. Your dog will follow your hand to the ground. Then slowly drag the treat or lure forward, she will start to move her paws forward. At the same time, gently apply pressure to the dog's shoulders. When your dog is in the down position say, "Good down," and give her a treat or lure.
- Before standing, gently hold your dog between the shoulder blades; place your left foot on the leash so your puppy cannot stand up, repeat, "Good down" and, "stay."

- To bring your dog out of the down position give another command like heel, sit or come.
- If you are ending your session release your dog with "okay."

There you go. You're set. It's easy isn't it? Have fun with your beloved dog. You're friends for life.

EILEEN AND TANK

A Final Word from Eileen

I've heard stories about the family dog being out of control from people wanting to get rid of them. They've asked me to take their dog. I was able to persuade them to train their dog and make changes at home.

A family dog is just that, a family dog. Everyone should be involved just like they are with other members of the family. Training is fun. Dogs bring a lot of joy and happiness. You make them happy and they will make you happy.

Go through this book with the family before you bring a puppy or dog into the house. Make up a family chore list and practice for a week or two as if you had a dog. If anyone complains that's a good sign you shouldn't get a dog.

Each time I start a new group or go to someone's home to train, I'm inspired by the commitment of the owners. As the weeks go by they tell me how much better their dog behaves and how smart he or she is. They're proud of their dog.

Follow the suggestions in this book and you will have an easy time raising your dog. In no time you will say, "My dog is an Angel Dog at Heart."

www.angeldogstraining.net

CPSIA information can be obtained
at www.ICGtesting.com
Printed in the USA
FSOW02n2139011116
26847FS